GREAT MOMENTS IN OLYMPIC HISTORY

Olympic Gymnastics

Adam B. Hofstetter

rosen publishing's
rosen central®

New York

For Sam

Published in 2007 by The Rosen Publishing Group, Inc.
29 East 21st Street, New York, NY 10010

Library of Congress Cataloging-in-Publication Data

Hofstetter, Adam B.
   Olympic Gymnastics / Adam B. Hofstetter.
       p. cm. — (Great moments in Olympic history)
   Includes bibliographical references and index.
   ISBN-13: 9781-4042-0968-8
   ISBN-10: 1-4042-0968-9 (library binding)
   1. Gymnasts—Biography—Juvenile literature. 2. Gymnastics—History—Juvenile literature. 3. Olympics—History—Juvenile literature. I. Title.
   GV460.H64 2007
   796.44—dc22
                                                    2006023338

Manufactured in the United States of America

On the cover: At the 1996 Olympic Games in Atlanta, Georgia, Dominique Moceanu, Kerri Strug, and Shannon Miller salute the crowd after receiving the gold medal for the team competition. Although she injured her ankle on her first attempt, Strug helped secure the victory with a heroic performance on the vault.

CONTENTS

CHAPTER 1

The History of Olympic Gymnastics

The first Olympics, held by the ancient Greeks in 776 B.C., were many things. They included religious worship, cultural celebrations, athletic festivals, and training exercises for the Greek armies. At first, a footrace was the only event. Over time, races of different lengths were added. Eventually other events were added, including boxing, chariot racing, horseback riding, and a pentathlon that included the discus throw, the javelin throw, long jump, running, and wrestling. The Greeks also played a sport called *pankration*, which was a mix of boxing, wrestling, and kicking. One sport the ancient Olympics did not have, though, was gymnastics.

The Birth of Olympic Gymnastics

The first modern Olympic Games were held in Athens, Greece, in 1896—1,500 years after the last ancient Olympic Games were held. Gymnastics is one of the few sports that have been included in every modern Olympics. The first Olympic gymnastics competition did not look very much like the ones we see today. Many of

Athletes at the first modern Olympics stand in rows on the field as fans fill the stadium seats. Gymnastics was one of many sports making its Olympic debut when Athens, Greece, hosted the first modern version of the Olympic Games in 1896.

the moves that we now see performed commonly by almost all world-class gymnasts had not been conceived of back then. Also, early gymnastics competition at the Olympics included several events that we now associate with track and field, such as pole vault, broad jump, shot put, and the 100-meter dash. They also included a rope climb and a stone heave, events that have since been completely eliminated from the Olympics. Track-and-field events were not fully removed from international gymnastics competitions until 1954.

Seventy-one gymnasts from eight countries competed in the first modern Olympics, and an amazing fifty-two of them were from Greece. The other competing nations included Germany, Great Britain, France, Switzerland, Denmark, Sweden, and Hungary. Germany dominated the gymnastics competitions, winning both team competitions and more than half of all individual medals. In fact, they were the only team that competed on the horizontal bar. German gymnast Hermann Weingärtner won four individual medals, while teammate Alfred Flatow won gold on the parallel bars and silver on the horizontal bar. Despite the overwhelming presence of the Germans, Switzerland's Louis Zutter managed to win three medals in gymnastics.

The United States and Olympic Gymnastics

The United States didn't compete in gymnastics at the Olympic level until the 1904 Olympic Games, which were held in St. Louis, Missouri. The 1904 Olympics had many problems. They were poorly organized, divided into 2 separate competitions, and spread out over several months. Also, many foreign athletes did not attend due to the high cost of international travel. That summer, St. Louis was also hosting the Louisiana Purchase World Exhibition—a celebration of the one hundredth anniversary of the Louisiana Purchase. Many of the Olympic events were featured as "sideshow" events of the World Expo, and some were confused with sporting events that had nothing to do with the Olympics. All 107 gymnasts at the first competition were American. The 33-

year-old George Eyser dominated the competition by winning six medals in eight events, despite having a wooden left leg. The second competition included international athletes. The U.S. team did not win any medals in that competition.

In 1932, the American men again took advantage of a lack of international competition, this time due to the Great Depression. Thirty-seven countries attended the 1932 Summer Olympics—which were held in Los Angeles, California—but only half as many athletes took part in the games as had during the 1928 Olympics in Amsterdam, Netherlands. With only a few athletes competing in each event, the U.S. gymnasts swept the medals for rope climbing, tumbling, and Indian clubs—events that were removed from the Olympics after 1932.

The 1936 Olympics, held in Berlin, Germany, marked the first time the Americans sent a women's gymnastics team to compete. The U.S. men's and women's teams both went home without any medals, but there were some positive stories. Several members of the women's gymnastic team were married to members of the men's team. Another couple from the two teams got married after the 1936 Olympics.

Up to 1948, Olympic events were always held outdoors. Competing outside was difficult for many athletes but especially for the gymnasts. Their balance was greatly affected by wind and other weather conditions. The 1948 Olympics were the first to hold some events—including gymnastics—indoors. Those games were held in London, England. The U.S. team decided to travel there by ship. Being on a boat that rocked and swayed in the ocean made gymnastic training practices very difficult. However, that might have helped, because the U.S. women's team won their first medal: a bronze in the team competition. The team was led by Helen Schifano, who placed second on the vault. It would be the last Olympic medal the American women would receive until 1984.

Rising Popularity

Before 1960, anyone who showed up at the U.S. Olympic Trials was allowed to compete. As gymnastics grew in popularity, the United States created a qualifying process in 1960. Under these new guidelines, gymnasts had to meet certain standards in order to be invited to the Olympic Trials.

Since then, Olympic gymnastics has continued to grow in popularity around the world. The greatest growth came in 1972, when the success and energy of Soviet gymnast Olga Korbut caught the world's attention. Gymnastics has enjoyed a huge following around the world since then and remains one of the most popular sports in the Olympics. The world's fascination with gymnastics grew even more in 1976, when Romanian Nadia Comaneci became the first gymnast to earn a perfect score in the Olympics.

Success for the U.S. Gymnasts

For more than 30 years, the Soviet team had dominated Olympic gymnastics. At the 1984 Summer Games in Los Angeles, California—with the Soviet Union and 13 other Communist countries boycotting the Olympics—American gymnasts finally gained international recognition. Both the men's and women's teams won several medals. Excelling on the parallel bars in the team competition, Mitch Gaylord became the first American to earn a perfect 10.00 at the Olympics, and Peter Vidmar received a 10.00 moments later on the pommel horse. On the women's side, Mary Lou Retton scored two perfect 10.00s in the floor exercise and the vault. She won a gold medal in the women's individual all-around competition plus four other medals.

Despite their success, a dark cloud hovered over U.S. gymnastics because the Americans had never

Mary Lou Retton performs her floor exercise routine at the 1984 Olympics. She became the first American gymnast to win the individual all-around gold medal at the Olympics. Retton's success at the 1984 games inspired countless American girls to take up gymnastics.

9

dominated a truly international Olympics. That finally changed in 1996. That year the Americans faced a strong field, including tough Russian and Romanian teams. They earned their first team gold thanks to the heroics of Kerri Strug, a relatively unknown gymnast. Strug's courageous performance on the vault, despite her badly injured ankle, cemented the U.S. victory.

In Athens in 2004, the U.S. team once again proved themselves worthy of competing on an international scale. Paul Hamm became the first and only American to win the men's individual all-around competition. This victory came after a fall in the vault event that was nearly disastrous and a debate over the scoring of another gymnast's routine.

Times Have Changed

Gymnastics has changed a lot since it appeared in the first modern Olympics more than 100 years ago. Old events have been replaced and new events have been introduced. Systems of judging and scoring continue to change. A spectator from the 1896 games would have a hard time recognizing many of today's events. Some Olympic moments, though, have been so significant that they can be appreciated by just about anyone. In the coming chapters, we'll take a closer look at some of the greatest moments for gymnasts in Olympic history.

German athlete Carl Schuhmann seemed to be everywhere during the 1896 Olympics. This image shows Schuhmann in his gold-medal performance on the long horse vault, an event that is somewhat similar to the pommel horse event seen in men's gymnastics today.

Schuhmann Does It All

Spectators at the 1896 Olympics certainly saw a lot of Carl Schuhmann. The German athlete was a member of the gymnastics squad that won both team medals. He added an individual gold medal on the vault. But that wasn't enough for Schuhmann. He also entered the weightlifting competition, where he tied for fourth place. He competed in three track-and-field events, where his best finish was fifth place in the triple jump. Still not satisfied with his accomplishments, Schuhmann also competed in wrestling, defeating weightlifting champion Launceston Elliot of Great Britain in the first round of competition. Despite being much smaller and lighter than most of the other wrestlers, Schuhmann made it to the gold-medal match, which lasted so long that it finally had to be postponed because it was too dark to see. When the match continued the next morning, Schuhmann won the gold medal. He became one of the most well-known athletes of the first modern Olympic Games.

CHAPTER 2

The "Munchkin of Munich": Olga Korbut

Prior to the 1972 Summer Olympics in Munich, Germany, gymnastics was popular in the Soviet Union and parts of Europe but was often ignored by the rest of the world. It was a sport performed by graceful women in their 20s and 30s, and not by the tiny, dynamic teenagers we see today.

In 1972, tiny Olga Korbut thrilled spectators and athletes at the Munich games with her surprisingly acrobatic moves on the balance beam and uneven bars. Korbut's energy and technical excellence were new developments in Olympic gymnastics. Thanks to her exciting, athletic, and innovative performance at the Munich games, Korbut turned the sport into an international sensation and changed gymnastics forever.

A Natural Gymnast

Olga Korbut was the youngest of four children born to an engineer and a cook in the Soviet town of Grodno, Belarus. Her natural athletic ability was evident at an early age. Inspired by an older sister who was a skilled gymnast, Korbut began her gymnastics training when she was just 8 years old. At the age of 11, she was studying under famous coach Renald Knysh, who soon became her personal coach.

Gymnastics had been similar to ballet prior to the 1972 Olympics. Korbut and Knysh brought explosive athleticism to a sport that, until they came along, had been rooted in fluidity and grace. Knysh taught Korbut the backward somersault (known as a back salto) on the balance beam. Such innovation was very controversial at the time. The move was thought by many to be too dangerous for female gymnasts. The National Soviet Sports Council criticized Olga's moves. In 1974, the International Federation of Gymnastics (FIG) considered banning her moves, but this never happened.

After performing successfully at several local and regional junior championships, Korbut quickly moved up to senior competition. When she was just 14 years old, she placed fifth in the 1969 Soviet championships, her first national competition. It was there that she first performed some of the groundbreaking moves that she became known for. The audience loved her and the judges recognized her talent, but the National Soviet Sports Council strongly disapproved. Her critics were soon silenced as she continued to improve her routines. A year later, at the same competition, she won gold in the vault event. By the time Korbut arrived at the Munich games in 1972, she was a confident, enthusiastic, and very talented 17-year-old gymnast.

On to Munich

During the team competition in Munich, Korbut's spectacular performance on the uneven bars turned her into an international star. In that routine, she showed off the first backward release move ever attempted on the uneven bars—a move so unusual and impressive that it became known as the Korbut Flip. She stood on the higher of the two bars, did a back handspring, and caught the bar on her way down. The Korbut Flip was soon

Here Korbut is shown during her daring and innovative balance beam routine at the 1972 Olympics. Moves she pioneered in Munich are still performed today by gymnasts everywhere.

System Reuther

14

copied by gymnasts everywhere, though it is no longer performed at the Olympics because standing on the high bar is now illegal. Her feat led the Soviet squad to a gold medal in the team competition. After the 1972 games, the adoring press nicknamed her the "Munchkin of Munich."

In the individual all-around competition, Korbut was again the best gymnast through the first two events. With the uneven bars next, she seemed to have the gold medal wrapped up. Just seconds into her routine, however, she stubbed her toes on the mat, and things only got worse from there. By the time it was over, Korbut had committed three errors and earned a score of only 7.50. She was out of the running for the individual all-around gold. The title went to her Soviet teammate Lyudmila Turischeva. Never afraid to show emotion, Korbut cried when she saw her low score. The hearts of viewers around the world melted.

Korbut rebounded in time to earn silver on the uneven bars. She also captured the gold for the floor exercise and the balance beam. Her gold-medal routine on the balance beam was breathtaking. She flawlessly executed seemingly impossible moves, including the back salto that she is credited with pioneering. Another part of her beam routine—a backward somersault to swingdown known as the Korbut Flick—is still performed by gymnasts in women's competitions worldwide.

Lyudmila Turischeva

In spite of her success and popularity, Olga Korbut may not have been the best gymnast in Munich. That distinction may have belonged to her teammate, Lyudmila Turischeva.

Korbut and Turischeva were as opposite as they could be. Korbut was outgoing and emotional; Turischeva was calm and businesslike. Korbut's performances were all about energy and innovation; Turischeva's were about technical excellence.

The 1972 games marked Turischeva's second trip to the Olympics, having won the team gold with her Soviet squad at the 1968 games. When Korbut debuted in Munich, Turischeva was the team leader and a decorated veteran who had won the individual all-around title at the 1970 World Championships.

She did not disappoint, calmly winning the all-around gold medal and taking a silver and bronze in individual events, in addition to sharing another team gold. After successfully defending her all-around title at the 1974 World Championships, she was back at the Olympics again in 1976, winning her third team gold medal. Even with a bad back, she managed to win silver medals in the vault and floor exercise and a bronze in the all-around. This brought her career Olympic medal total to an incredible nine medals.

Her most famous performance, though, came at the 1975 World Cup competition in London, England. As she finished her dismount from the uneven bars, a metal hook that was supporting the bars broke and the entire apparatus came crashing loudly to the ground. The crowd was stunned but Turischeva, ever the professional, never flinched. She saluted the judges and moved on without even turning around to see what had happened. She went on to win not just the all-around competition but also every individual apparatus, showcasing the self-control for which she was so well-known.

International Star

The global fame Korbut earned for herself and for women's gymnastics in general did not fade when the Olympics ended. She received so much fan mail that her local post office in Belarus assigned a special clerk to handle it all. When she became the youngest person ever to be awarded the Soviet Union's title of Honored Master of Sport, it was clear that she had won over her critics as well.

Korbut's success in competition continued. In 1973, she won a national competition, took a silver medal in the individual all-around competition at the European Championships, and was named "Female Athlete of the Year" by the Associated Press, a major international news organization. At the 1974 World Championships, she showed that she was still one of the

Here, Olga Korbut performs a "Korbut Flip" at the 1972 Olympics. It was Korbut's dangerous and acrobatic performance on the uneven bars that won the hearts of gymnastics fans everywhere and catapulted the sport to new heights of popularity.

17

world's best gymnasts by winning six medals in six events, including gold medals in the vault event and the team competition.

Success in Montreal

When Korbut arrived at the 1976 Summer Olympics in Montreal, Canada, she was a superstar and leader of a talented Soviet team. They were facing their toughest challenge in years from an up-and-coming Romanian squad. At 21, Korbut's gymnastic career was nearing its end. Spectators crowded into the arena to see their beloved "Munchkin" take flight for perhaps the last time. They were not disappointed. Despite a historic performance from the talented young Romanian Nadia Comaneci during the team competition, Korbut helped the Soviets win another Olympic team gold.

In her best event—the balance beam—Korbut delivered another outstanding performance that wowed both the crowd and the judges. In past Olympics, her scores of 9.825 and 9.90 would have been enough to win gold. This time, however, Comaneci performed even better on the beam and won the gold. Korbut still captured second place and an amazing sixth Olympic medal.

Life After Gymnastics

With so many memorable and exciting performances behind her, Korbut retired from competition. She earned a degree from a university in Grodno the following year and married a popular musician from Belarus. She gave birth to a son in 1979. As Korbut's career was winding down, the rising star of Nadia Comaneci caught the world's attention. But it was Korbut who truly changed the face of gymnastics. Her success in Munich and the resulting media attention brought worldwide recognition to a sport that had been largely overlooked up to that point. Inspired by Korbut's daring moves, thousands of young girls flocked to gymnastics classes, helping the sport grow. Many of them became talented gymnasts who dominated the sport in the years to come. Korbut also helped change the sport's focus from artistry and style to athleticism and acrobatics. More than 7,100 athletes competed in the 1972 Summer Olympics, but none of them had a more lasting impact than Olga Korbut, the "Munchkin of Munich."

The Soviet women's team shows off their medals from the Munich Olympics. Korbut, noticeably smaller than the rest of her teammates, is in the center. Turischeva stands to the left of Korbut.

CHAPTER 3

Perfection! Nadia Comaneci

The year was 1976. No gymnast, male or female, had ever received a perfect score in any Olympic event in the 80-year history of the modern Olympic games. Near-perfect scores such as 9.90 (the highest score earned at the previous Olympics) were hard enough to achieve. A 10.00 was thought to be completely out of reach. However, a 14-year-old girl from Romania was about to change all that.

Romanian gymnast Nadia Comaneci stunned the crowd, judges, and athletes when she scored a perfect 10.00 on the uneven bars at the 1976 Olympic Games in Montreal, Canada. By the time she had scored her seventh perfect 10.00, everyone watching knew they had witnessed one of the greatest gymnastic performances in Olympic history.

Rising Star

No discussion of Olympic gymnastics would be complete without mentioning Nadia Comaneci. Born in Romania in November 1961 and named after a character in a Russian movie, Comaneci was just 6 years old when she got her start in gymnastics. She performed all over Romania with her hometown gymnastics team when she was just 9 years old. At age 13, she won four gold medals (including the individual all-around title) at the 1975 European Championships in Norway. She also won the individual all-around title at the pre-Olympics competition in Montreal, Canada, later that same year and was named "Athlete of the Year" by the Associated Press. She won the European Championships again in 1977.

A Perfect 10.00!

By the 1976 Summer Olympics in Montreal, the 14-year-old was ready to perform on the biggest stage of all. With young talents like Nellie Kim, Lyudmila Turischeva, and Olga Korbut, the Soviet women's team was as powerful as ever. Comaneci was already a star gymnast and was expected to give the Soviets some stiff competition. She did much more than that. By the time the games were over, all anyone could talk about was Comaneci's historic performance. In her strongest events, she didn't merely perform better than every gymnast in Montreal—she performed better than every gymnast in Olympic history.

First came the uneven bars, an event in which gymnasts swing themselves over and around two bars set at different heights. Gymnasts are required to perform a set number of spins, flips, turns, and moves from one bar to the other before finally hurling themselves off the higher bar, doing more twists and somersaults in the air, and finally landing. The more difficult the combination of moves, and the better they are executed, the higher the scores will be.

In her routine, Comaneci performed a dismount that she invented, starting below the higher of the two bars, swinging up, and doing a forward somersault in the air while twisting her body around. In gymnastics terms, the move is known as a "kip to front salto." However, it has become known as the Comaneci salto. It is rated as one of the most difficult skills, and only a few gymnasts in the world have performed it successfully.

When Comaneci finished her routine, she and coach Bela Karolyi knew she had earned a high score. In fact, her score was so high that it didn't even fit on the scoreboard. Because nobody had ever earned a perfect score at the Olympics, the scoreboards had only enough spaces to display scores up to 9.99. With no room for the extra digit, the scoreboard displayed Comaneci's 10.00 as a 1.00. According to several reports, she and Karolyi were horrified when they saw the 1.00, but soon realized what had happened. Comaneci easily won the gold medal in that event and made history with her perfect score.

Bela Karolyi

Bela Karolyi is considered by many to be the best gymnastics coach ever to appear in the Olympics. Throughout his long career, Karolyi has coached many successful Olympic gymnasts, including Nadia Comaneci, Mary Lou Retton, Kim Zmeskal, Kerri Strug, and Dominique Moceanu.

Karolyi established a gymnastics school in Romania during the late 1960s. He selected the young girls who would attend the school, and personally trained the cream of the crop. Karolyi led the Romanian women's Olympic team to greatness in 1976 with the help of his superstar gymnast, Nadia Comaneci. Due to his success, Karolyi was named head coach of the Romanian team for the 1980 Olympics.

Disputes between Karolyi and the Romanian Gymnastics Federation led Karolyi to move to the United States with his wife, Marta, in 1981. They opened a gym in Houston, Texas, which struggled at first but soon found success. Many hopeful gymnasts wanted to train with the coach who guided Comaneci to her perfect 10.00s. Karolyi coached Mary Lou Retton and Julianne McNamara at the 1984 Olympics, both of whom won multiple medals. Thanks to their success, Karolyi was hired as head coach of the U.S. women's gymnastics team for the 1988 Olympics.

Before retiring from coaching Olympians in 1996, Karolyi led U.S. gymnasts to thirteen Olympic medals. In 1997, Karolyi was inducted into the International Gymnastics Hall of Fame. Today he is remembered for his rigorous yet successful training regimen and his many star students.

Karolyi watches in the background as Comaneci (second from right) walks with her Romanian teammates. Comaneci's performance at the 1976 Olympics brought both of them fame, and Karolyi has gone on to coach many successful Olympians.

23

An elated Comaneci gestures to the crowd as the scoreboard displays only a 1.00 for her fantastic performance on the uneven bars. Scoreboards for future competitions were modified to be able to display scores of 10.00.

A Daring Performance on the Beam

The next event was the balance beam, considered one of gymnastics' most difficult events. Olga Korbut, who delighted the world with her beam routine at the 1972 games, returned to defend her gold medal. Comaneci knew that a great performance simply would not be enough for gold. She performed flawless backflips, handstands, and twists, showing judges and spectators a graceful, artistic, and technically masterful performance. Her routine was most notable for its originality, including yet another move that Comaneci had invented.

Imagine how hard it would be to do a cartwheel on a 4-inch-wide beam. Now imagine how much harder it would be to do that cartwheel without using your hands. In gymnastics, this is called an aerial walkover. Before Comaneci's balance beam routine, nobody had ever done such a thing. Comaneci's aerial walkover was the world's first on the balance beam. Comaneci again shocked the world with her perfection. She received another perfect score and her second gold medal. With Korbut settling for silver, Comaneci's victory on the beam made her the new darling of the international gymnastics community.

That was hardly the end. Continuing to showcase a perfect blend of artistry, athleticism, and self-control, Comaneci earned a total of seven perfect scores, thoroughly dominating the competition. In six events, including the team competition, Comaneci won five medals: gold in the individual all-around, balance beam, and uneven bars; a bronze in the floor exercise; and a team silver.

Unstoppable

The following year, Comaneci won the individual all-around title at the European Championships once again. She also won a gold medal on the balance beam at the 1978 World Championships. In 1979, she won the European individual all-around title yet again. She was leading at the World Championships before being hospitalized for blood poisoning due to a cut on her wrist from her metal grip buckle. She defied doctors and left the hospital to compete on the balance beam, earning a 9.95 and helping the Romanians win their first ever team gold.

Once Comaneci made history with the first Olympic 10.00, gymnastics suddenly became the hottest ticket in town. Events sold out, and soon people were paying more than five times the face value for tickets to see the 86-pound (39-kg) wonder perform. She made it worth every penny.

1980 Summer Olympics

Four years after her first Olympics, Comaneci returned to represent Romania at the 1980 Summer Games in Moscow, Russia. Her historic performance in 1976 had brought Romanian gymnastics newfound respect and admiration. Better funding for the program was already paying off. This time Comaneci led a much more talented and experienced Romanian team. For the first time in Olympic history, Romanian women medaled in every individual event.

The Soviets again had a strong team, and they proved it by winning yet another team gold. Nellie Kim added another gold by tying with Comaneci for first place in the floor exercise, and other Soviet gymnasts won gold in the vault event and the individual all-around. But the Romanians did well, too. On the uneven bars, Romanians Emilia Eberle and Melita Ruhn took silver and bronze, and Ruhn also won bronze in the vault event. In addition to her shared gold in the floor exercise, Comaneci was again dominant on the balance beam, winning yet another gold medal. She tied for silver in the individual all-around and led the Romanians to silver in the team competition. With her two gold medals and two silvers at the 1980 games to add to the five medals she earned in Montreal, Comaneci cemented her place among the greatest athletes of the twentieth century.

Nadia Comaneci Today

Today Comaneci lives in Oklahoma with her husband, 1984 Olympic gold medal gymnast Bart Connor. Long since retired as a gymnast, she remains active in the sport. She and her husband own the Bart Connor Gymnastics Academy and several sports equipment stores. They publish *International Gymnast* magazine and work as television commentators for many gymnastics competitions. In addition, Comaneci serves as vice-chair of the Board of Directors of the Special Olympics and is honorary president of the Romanian Gymnastics Federation and the Romanian Olympic Committee. She is also Romania's Ambassador of Sports, a member of the International Gymnastics Federation Foundation, and has received two Olympic Order awards from the International Olympic Committee (IOC). Outside of sports, Comaneci is the vice president of the Board of Directors of the Muscular Dystrophy Association and spoke at the United Nations to launch the Year 2000 International Year of Volunteers. She has started a charity in Romania to help orphaned children. She and her husband had their first child, a boy named Dylan, in June 2006.

CHAPTER 4

American "Munchkins": Mary Lou Retton and Kerri Strug

Until 1984, no American woman had won an individual Olympic medal in gymnastics. The only medal the American women had ever won was the team bronze in 1948. Some people discount the medals won by the United States in the 1984 Olympics because they did not compete against the Soviets. The Soviets boycotted the games in retaliation for a U.S. boycott of the 1980 Moscow games. But American gymnast Mary Lou Retton still faced some stiff competition at the 1984 games in Los Angeles, California, especially from the heavily favored Romanian Ecaterina Szabo. Retton responded not simply by winning America's first gymnastics medal since 1948, but by dominating the competition in a way that U.S. gymnasts had never done before.

Watching Nadia Comaneci

Born in West Virginia and inspired by watching Nadia Comaneci on television, Retton enrolled in her first gymnastics class at the age of 7. She proved to be exceedingly talented. Before long she was being coached by the very same Bela Karolyi who had coached Comaneci to a perfect performance in 1976. Retton—all 4 feet, 9 inches (144.8 cm) of her—soon emerged as one of the best gymnasts in the country, but a wrist injury forced her to miss the 1983 World Championships. Soon after this, she injured her knee. Retton had knee surgery 6 weeks before the 1984 Olympics, but recovered in time to compete.

Stealing First Place

With the games being held on American soil and without the normally strong Soviets, the home crowd was expecting great things from the U.S. team, and they were not disappointed. From swimming to track and field, Americans dominated many events at the 1984 Summer Games. Retton was determined to make sure that gymnastics was no different. When the individual all-around competition started, Retton gave the type of performance everyone knew she was capable of. She excelled on the uneven bars and the balance beam. However, Szabo's routines were even better. With just two events to go in the individual all-around competition, Retton was trailing Szabo for the gold.

Retton salutes the crowd as she finishes her gold-medal floor exercise routine at the 1984 Olympics. It was just one of five medals she won at the Los Angeles games.

Up next was the floor exercise. Retton turned in the performance of a lifetime. A fantastic succession of flips, jumps, and somersaults led to a perfect 10.00. Even so, Retton was still in second place by a hair going into the last rotation. Her final event was the vault, and only another perfect 10.00 would put her ahead of Szabo. The vault she chose to attempt was called a double Tsukahara. It was difficult enough to earn the 10.00 she needed—if she performed it perfectly. She hit the vault, spun through the air, and stuck the landing, smiling triumphantly at the adoring crowd. Sure enough, she received her second perfect 10.00 of the competition, passing Szabo by just 0.05 of a point. Retton became the first woman outside of Eastern Europe to win the individual all-around title.

Amazing Mary Lou Retton

Retton did not just win the individual all-around gold, but also a silver and two bronze medals in individual events. She led the American squad to a silver medal in the team competition. Her historic five-medal performance tied Comaneci's record for a single Olympics. Her enthusiasm and spirit won the hearts of Americans. The praise did not end there. *Sports Illustrated* named her "Sportswoman of the Year." She was voted the Women's Sports Foundation Athlete of the Year for 1984. Wheaties cereal put her in their "Wheaties Hall of Champions" and made her the first woman to appear on a Wheaties box. Many joked that Retton was so small that the cereal-box picture was actually life-sized.

The following year, Retton became a member of the United States Olympic Committee (USOC) Olympic Hall of Fame. She decided to use her fame as a way to speak to the country about political issues. At the height of her popularity, she retired from gymnastics and became a motivational speaker and "fitness ambassador." She had small parts in a few movies and was a television announcer for the 1988 Summer Olympics.

During the 1990s, Retton's star still did not fade. A 1993 survey by the Associated Press named her the Most Popular Athlete in America. The following year, the USOC named an award for athletic excellence after her. A year later, the Women's Sports Foundation awarded her the Flo Hyman Award for her "dignity,

Mary Lou Retton's Media

If you've never seen Retton's gold-medal performance, you can still catch her on one of her many other television appearances. In addition to doing television coverage for gymnastics competitions, she hosts the annual telethon for the Children's Miracle Network. She has also guest-starred on many television shows and appeared in the movies *Scrooged* and *Naked Gun 33$\frac{1}{3}$*. In 2000, she took a brief break from television to write a book that shares her positive attitude and stresses determination and teamwork. In 2001, it was back to TV as she coproduced and starred in *Mary Lou's Flip Flop Shop*, a children's television show on PBS that emphasized fitness and exercise.

spirit, and commitment to excellence." In 1997, 13 years after her triumph in Los Angeles, she was inducted into the International Gymnastics Hall of Fame.

Following Mary Lou Retton

Regardless of whether the Soviet team was present when Retton won the individual all-around title, her victory inspired countless young American girls to believe that they could one day do the same. One of them was Kerri Strug, who was 6 years old when Retton dominated gymnastics at the 1984 Olympics. "My dream was to be an all-around champion like Mary Lou Retton," Strug says on her official Web site. At age 13, she already mirrored Retton's small size. She made the tough decision to chase her dream of competing in the Olympics some day, even though it meant moving away from home to train with Bela Karolyi in Houston, Texas.

Strug made the U.S. Olympic team less than 2 years later. As the youngest member of the American squad, Strug won a team bronze at the 1992 Olympics in Barcelona, Spain, when she was just 14 years old. Strug was a rising star in American gymnastics and had high hopes for the 1996 Olympics in Atlanta, Georgia. However, her career was almost cut short by an injury 2 years before the Atlanta games. At a small competition in Arizona, she suffered a terrible fall from the uneven bars that left her with a serious back injury. Despite a lengthy and difficult rehabilitation, Strug made it back to the U.S. team in time to help them place third at the 1995 World Championships. Strug and the women's team were ready for the 1996 Olympics.

Team Gold for the United States

The year 1996 marked the first Olympics held in the United States since Retton became a star at the 1984 games. The home crowd was again expecting big things, especially from the U.S. women's gymnastics team, which had been nicknamed "The Magnificent Seven." In the team competition, they battled the Russian squad for first place and had a lead going into the last rotation. All they needed for victory was a good score in the vault event from either of their last two gymnasts. This would clinch the country's first ever team gold.

One of the biggest U.S. stars, Dominique Moceanu, was up next, but she fell on her first attempt. Most of the 40,000 fans in attendance thought she would nail the next one and seal the victory. However, Moceanu fell again on her second attempt. The U.S. team now needed a solid vault from Strug. She, too, fell on her first attempt. When it became clear that she had hurt her ankle in the fall, it looked as if the American women might have to settle for silver.

Karolyi took Strug aside and gave her a quick pep talk. Strug limped to the runway for her second attempt. It didn't look like she'd be able to run to the vault, let alone stick her landing on the other side of it—if she could even jump well enough to get to the other side of it. But that's just what she did. Strug flew over the vault and landed perfectly, ensuring the gold medal with an impressive score of 9.712. Standing on one foot, she raised her arms to the adoring crowd and hopped around to salute the judges. Then Strug crumpled to the floor in horrible pain.

In one of the lasting images of the 1996 games, Karolyi scooped up the tiny Strug and carried her off in his arms while the crowd cheered wildly. Karolyi also helped her onto the medal stand so she could receive the reward for her courageous victory along with the rest of her team. Her injury—two torn ligaments in her ankle—prevented her from competing in the individual events, but her courage made her an instant sports hero. Her picture was on a Wheaties box and the cover of *Sports Illustrated*. She was also invited to the White House to meet President Clinton.

This photograph of Karolyi carrying the injured Strug away from the medal stand after her successful vault became one of the most enduring images from the 1996 Olympics.

Tiny Heroes

Just as with Mary Lou Retton's win 12 years earlier, Strug's performance had come down to the vault, and she came through for her team. The two tiny gymnasts will be remembered for years to come for their incredible performances under pressure.

Catching Up with Kerri Strug

After the 1996 Olympics, Strug performed in the Magic of MGM/Ice Capades and Disney's World On Ice. She officially announced her retirement in 1996 and enrolled in college in California. After earning a bachelor's degree and a master's degree, she became an elementary school teacher before moving into politics. In 2005, President Bush appointed her to a job at the Justice Department. Millions of fans around the world will always remember her as the brave gymnast who gritted her teeth through pain and brought home victory.

CHAPTER 5

The Comeback: Paul Hamm

After three rounds of the men's individual all-around competition at the 2004 Summer Olympics in Athens, Greece, American gymnast Paul Hamm was in first place and in good position to give the United States its first Olympic title in the event. Then disaster struck. Hamm missed his landing in the vault event so badly that he nearly knocked over the judges' bench as he fell. In fact, if the bench had not been there to stop him, Hamm might have fallen off the platform entirely and been injured. His standing in the competition fell along with him. He suddenly found himself in twelfth place. At that moment, it looked like Hamm's shot at an individual medal was gone.

Gymnastics: It's in the Blood

It was hardly the situation Hamm imagined when he took up gymnastics as a 7-year-old back in his hometown of Waukesha, Wisconsin. Gymnastics was a family affair for Hamm, whose twin brother, Morgan, competed on the U.S. Olympic team along with him. After seeing their sister Betsy take lessons, the twins wanted to learn, too. Their father put a steel high bar in the backyard along with a homemade pommel horse and set of parallel bars. They joined a local gym and hooked up with coach Stacy

Paul (above) and Morgan Hamm may be the most athletically gifted twin brothers in American history. Here they are at the 2000 U.S. Olympic Trials.

Maloney, who was still their coach when they performed in the 2000 Olympics.

The Hamm brothers were an immediate success, soon making it to the U.S. Junior National Team. Paul made it in 1995, and Morgan made it in 1996. At the U.S. Junior National Championships in 1998, Paul tied for first on the still rings, and also won three silver medals. Their junior team won the international championship that year and again in 1999, with Paul taking the 1999 individual all-around title. That year, Paul moved to the senior team, and his brother Morgan joined him in 2000. Paul placed third at the National Championships in 2000, but just fourteenth in the individual all-around competition at the 2000 Olympics in Sydney, Australia. Morgan's best finish in Sydney was seventh place in the floor exercise, and the U.S. squad came in fifth overall. It was a disappointing showing for the Hamm brothers and the entire U.S. team.

If his first Olympic performance was a learning experience, then Paul Hamm certainly showed himself to be a good student. He earned a seventh-place finish in the individual all-around competition at the 2001 World Championships and established himself as one of the world's best gymnasts. He continued to improve, and in 2003 he won the individual all-around title at the World Championships, a first for American male gymnasts.

Paul and Morgan Hamm

Sibling rivalry is one thing, but competing against your twin brother at the Olympics is quite another. Paul Hamm and his twin brother, Morgan, both competed at the 2000 and 2004 Olympics. They are the first twins to make a U.S. Olympic gymnastics team. That honor almost went to twins Dennis and Dan Hayden, who competed at the 1988 Olympic Trials, but failed to make the team. The only other siblings to make the U.S. gymnastics squad were Jack and Richard Beckner, brothers who were on the 1956 Olympic team.

Hamm's outstanding performance on the pommel horse at the 2004 Summer Olympics, shown here, put him in the lead shortly before his disastrous fall on the vault. Hamm earned a 9.70 for his routine, moving him into fourth place in the individual all-around competition.

Ups and Downs in Athens

The 2004 Olympics looked, at first, to be a continuation of Hamm's success. He jumped out to a lead of 0.038 point over his biggest rival, Chinese gymnast Yang Wei, after the first three rotations. Then came his disastrous fall on the vault. Hamm had chosen to perform a particularly challenging vault, one that was rated 9.9 out of 10 in difficulty and included a blind landing. Nevertheless, he had never missed a vault landing in competition and had every reason to believe that this one would be no exception. However, he didn't get enough height to complete the two-and-a-half twists before landing. The crowd gasped as he—and his Olympic hopes—came crashing down.

The embarrassing crash left him visibly dazed for a moment, but then Hamm picked himself up and moved on. There were two rotations left. He could still turn in a strong performance and maybe even win a bronze medal. Up next for Hamm were the parallel bars. With a succession of perfect handstands, artful flips, and a flawless dismount, he scored an impressive 9.837. However, he had performed first in that round, and good routines from the other gymnasts could keep him from winning a medal.

Next, China's Yang Wei performed on the high bar. After missing a grab, he fell from the bar and was suddenly out of the competition for the gold. Japan's Isao Yoneda fell, too. Ioan Suciu and Marian Dragulescu of Romania both faltered. Thanks to his outstanding performance and the mistakes of other gymnasts, Hamm was back in fourth place when it was his turn for the last apparatus: the high bar.

Hamm excelled on the high bar. Holding on with only one hand, he spun around and around the bar, faster and faster, looking just as confident and in control with one hand as others did with two. Then came three straight blind release moves, which he completed perfectly by throwing his body up and over the bar and catching the bar again on the way down, each time flying higher than the last. His dismount and landing were just as impressive. He threw his fists into the air triumphantly before waving to the thunderous crowd. After a big hug from his coach, Hamm could only sit and wait for his score, knowing that he needed a 9.825 for the gold. Hamm and the crowd erupted when the scoreboard flashed a 9.837, which won him the gold medal by the smallest margin in the history of Olympic gymnastics. Hamm had become the first American man to win the individual all-around gold.

Not So Fast…

Unfortunately for Hamm, it wasn't over. After the meet, the scoring that led to Hamm's medal was challenged. The bronze medalist, South Korean Yang Tae-young, complained that the start value of his parallel bars routine (determined by the difficulty of the routine) should have been 0.1 point higher. With the final standings so close, that 0.1 point made the difference between first place and third for Yang.

The FIG agreed that Yang should have been awarded a higher start value, and they suspended three judges. The USOC backed Hamm, quoting an Olympic rule that states that scores must be disputed the day of the event. Additionally, Yang had made an undetected error on the parallel bars that should have resulted in a 0.2 penalty. This would have knocked Yang out of medal contention entirely. Yang's camp, though, argued that the deduction

41

would have applied to many gymnasts but was not taken off their scores either.

The FIG finally declared that the results of the event would stand. However, they sent a letter to the USOC suggesting that Hamm voluntarily give his gold medal to Yang as "the ultimate demonstration of fair play." The USOC responded angrily that Hamm was not responsible for cleaning up the FIG's messes. They refused to deliver the letter to Hamm.

Code of Points

As every competitive gymnast knows, the Code of Points is a comprehensive list of skills and elements and their difficulty levels. Separate versions of the code are produced for artistic gymnastics, rhythmic gymnastics, sports acrobatics, sports aerobics, and trampolining. Published by the FIG, the code acts as a scoring manual for all gymnasts and judges. The Code of Points is usually updated after every Summer Olympics to include new skills that have been performed, add or subtract value to existing skills, and make any necessary changes to the rules. Similarly, minor changes are often made every year after the World Championships.

However, after the Hamm controversy in 2004, the FIG scrapped the Code of Points and the entire scoring system for a completely new version that came out in 2006. There has been much debate over the new code. Some believe that it is a necessary step toward fairer and more objective judging. Others argue that it will be too confusing to people outside the gymnastics community and lead to a loss of interest in the sport. Both sides agree that the new code may eliminate the possibility of scoring a perfect 10.00.

Finally...Victory!

Eventually Yang went to the Court of Arbitration for Sport (CAS), an independent international organization that settles sports-related disputes. Hamm traveled to Switzerland for the hearing, which lasted more than 11 hours. Finally, almost a month later and nearly 2 full months after Hamm first won the disputed gold medal, the CAS upheld the original results. Hamm could finally relax, knowing that the medal was his forever.

The joy and relief is evident on Hamm's face as he triumphantly salutes the crowd after winning the individual all-around gold medal by the slimmest margin in Olympic history. Hamm's improbable comeback made him the first American man to win the event.

Timeline

776 B.C. The first Olympics are held in ancient Greece. A footrace is the only event.

1896 The first modern Olympics are held in Athens, Greece.

1904 American gymnasts compete in the Olympics for the first time.

1932 Due in part to low international turnout, the U.S. sweeps the medals in several events.

1936 For the first time, the United States sends a women's gymnastics team to the Olympics.

1948 At the first Olympics to hold some events indoors, the U.S. women's team wins its first medal—a team bronze.

1954 Track-and-field events are removed from international gymnastics competition.

1960 The United States institutes a qualifying process for its Olympic gymnastics teams.

1972 Olga Korbut earns four medals and the adoration of millions of fans with her performance at the Munich Olympics.

1976 Romanian gymnast Nadia Comaneci scores the first 10.00 in Olympic history.

1984 With Soviet countries boycotting the Olympics, American gymnasts dominate the competition. American Mary Lou Retton wins the country's first individual all-around gold medal.

1996 After a miraculous vault by Kerri Strug, the American women win their first team gold at the Olympics in Atlanta, Georgia.

2004 Paul Hamm comes back from a shocking crash to become the first American man to win the Olympic individual all-around title.

Glossary

apparatus A piece of equipment used in artistic gymnastics.

arbitration A method of settling a legal dispute out of court.

balance beam A beam 10 centimeters wide, 500 centimeters long, and 120 centimeters above the floor. A performance on the beam lasts 70 to 90 seconds, includes an assortment of moves, and ends with a dismount.

boycott To protest the actions of an organization or country by refusing to have dealings with it.

deduction Points that judges take off a gymnast's score for errors. Most deductions are set by the Code of Points.

dignity A sense of pride and self-respect.

dismount To leave the apparatus at the end of the routine, usually with a final flip or salto.

floor exercise A gymnastic event performed by men and women that includes tumbling and other acrobatic moves on a mat 40 feet by 40 feet.

horizontal bar A bar 240 centimeters long, 2.8 centimeters in diameter, and 275 centimeters above the floor. Sometimes called the high bar.

innovation Something new and original.

Justice Department A department of the U.S. government designed to enforce laws and make sure they are administered fairly.

kip A move that brings the gymnast from below a bar to above it.

ligament A band of strong tissue that connects bones, muscles, and other body parts.

parallel bars Two bars side by side that are 350 centimeters long and 195 centimeters above the floor. They are positioned 42 to 52 centimeters apart.

pommel horse A padded apparatus 35 centimeters wide, 160 centimeters long, and 115 centimeters above the floor. On the top, it has two pommels, which look like big handles, set 40 to 45 centimeters apart.

rehabilitation Help given to someone who has been injured for the purpose of making them well.

rotation A regular or planned series of events.

salto A flip or somersault in which the feet come up over the head and the body rotates around the axis of the waist.

Soviet Relating to the former Soviet Union. Today, much of what was the Soviet Union is known as Russia.

telethon A televised broadcast that combines entertainment with appeals to donate money to a particular charity.

uneven bars Two bars side by side that are 150 centimeters apart on metal posts at different heights. The lower bar is 148 centimeters above the floor, and the higher bar is 228 centimeters above the floor.

vault A leaping action performed on the vaulting horse.

For More Information

International Federation of Gymnastics (FIG)
Rue des Oeuches 10
Case postale 359
2740 Moutier 1
Switzerland
Phone: 41-32-494-64-10
Email: info@fig-gymnastics.org
Web site: http://www.fig-gymnastics.com

International Gymnastics Hall of Fame
120 N. Robinson E-Concourse
Oklahoma City, OK 73102
Phone: 405-235-5600
Email: contact@ighof.com
Web site: http://www.ighof.com

International Olympic Committee (IOC)
Château de Vidy
1007 Lausanne
Switzerland
Phone: 41-21-621-61-11
Web site: http://www.olympic.org

National Collegiate Athletics Association (NCAA)
700 W. Washington Street
P.O. Box 6222
Indianapolis, IN 46206-6222
Phone: 317-917-6222
Web site: http://www.ncaa.org

United States Association of Independent Gymnastics Clubs, Inc.
Competition and Events Office
450 North End Avenue, Suite 20F
New York, NY 10282
Phone: 212-227-9792
Email: USAIGCPSNY2@aol.com
Web site: http://www.usaigc.com

USA Gymnastics
Pan Am Plaza, Suite 300
201 S. Capitol Avenue
Indianapolis, IN 46225
Phone: 317-237-5050
Email: webmaster@usa-gymnastics.org
Web site: http://www.usa-gymnastics.org

Web Sites

Due to the changing nature of Internet links, the Rosen Publishing Group, Inc., has developed an online list of Web sites related to the subject of this book. This site is updated regularly. Please use this link to access the list: **http://www.rosenlinks.com/gmoh/gymn**

For Further Reading

Bader, Amanda. *Paul and Morgan Hamm: Olympic Heroes.* New York: Razorbill, 2004.
Cohen, Joel H. *Superstars of Women's Gymnastics.* New York: Chelsea House Publishers, 1997.
Jackman, Joan. *Superguides: Gymnastics.* New York: DK Children, 2000.
Lessa, Christina. *Gymnastics Balancing Acts.* New York: Universe Books, 1997.
Strug, Kerri. *Heart of Gold.* Lanham, MD: Taylor Trade Publishing, 1996.
USA Gymnastics. *I Can Do Gymnastics.* New York: McGraw-Hill, 1993.

Bibliography

Comaneci, Nadia. *Nadia: The Autobiography of Nadia Comaneci.* London, England: X-S Books, 1981.

Hamm Twins. April 15, 2006. Retrieved August 7, 2006. (http://www.hammtwins.com)

Karolyi, Bela, and Nancy Ann Richardson. *Feel No Fear: The Power, Passion, and Politics of a Life in Gymnastics.* New York: Hyperion, 1996.

Mary Lou Retton. "Biography." Retrieved August 7, 2006. (http://www.marylouretton.com)

Nadia Comaneci.com. Retrieved August 7, 2006. (http://www.nadiacomaneci.com/bio.htm)

Olga Korbut Enterprises, Inc. "Biography." Retrieved August 7, 2006. (http://www.olgakorbut.com/biogr.htm)

Pound, Richard W. *Inside the Olympics: A Behind-the-Scenes Look at the Politics, the Scandals, and the Glory of the Games.* Hoboken, NJ: John Wiley & Sons, 2004.

Powers, John, Bela Karolyi, and Mary Lou Retton. *Mary Lou: Creating an Olympic Champion.* New York: McGraw-Hill, 1985.

Schaffer, Kay, and Sidonie Smith, eds. *The Olympics at the Millennium: Power, Politics and the Games.* Piscataway, NJ: Rutgers University Press, 2000.

Spivey, Nigel. *The Ancient Olympics: A History.* Oxford, England: Oxford University Press, 2004.

Strug, Kerri, and John P. Lopez. *Landing on My Feet: A Diary of Dreams.* Kansas City, MO: Andrews McMeel, 1997.

Strug, Kevin, and Karen Strug. "In the Wink of an Eye." April 30, 2005. Retrieved August 7, 2006. (http://www.strug.org/Pages/DayinLife.html)

Supponey, Michael. *Olga Korbut: A Biographical Portrait.* New York: Doubleday, 1975.

Wallechinsky, David. *The Complete Book of the Summer Olympics: Athens 2004 Edition.* Toronto, Canada: SportClassic Books, 2004.

Young, David C. *A Brief History of the Olympic Games.* Oxford, England: Blackwell Publishing, 2004.

Index

About the Author

Adam Hofstetter is a weekly columnist for SportsIllustrated.com. This is his third book for Rosen Publishing. When he's not attending various sports events, Adam can be found in Cedarhurst, New York, where he lives with his wife, Sarah, and their two children, Abby and Sam.

Photo Credits

Cover (Kerri Strug) © Doug Pensinger/Getty Images; cover, back cover, interior (background) © Shutterstock; p. 5 © Hulton Archive/Getty Images; pp. 9, 30 © Steve Powell/Getty Images; p. 11 © IOC/Olympic Museum/Allsport; p. 14 © Staff/AFP/Getty Images; pp. 17, 19 © Keystone/Getty Images; p. 23 © Tony Duffy/Allsport; p. 24 © AFP/Getty Images; p. 35 © Mike Powell/Allsport; p. 37 © Doug Pensinger/Allsport; pp. 39, 43 © Donald Miralle/Getty Images.

Designer: Michael J. Flynn
Editor: Greg Roza